Manuel de Falla's House and Museum

Centro Cultural Manuel de Falla

Public Foundation of
Granada City
Council

Department of Archives,
Libraries and Museums

... You cannot imagine how glad I was to accomplish this longawaited journey, and to spend some days together in wonderful Granada. (1919)

Introduction.

Mª Isabel de Falla

After my father's death in 1959, my Aunt María del Carmen decided not to return to Granada, which she had left in 1939 to accompany my uncle Manuel on his journey to the Argentine. We thought that there could be no better place to leave Manuel's belongings than in his house, just as they used to be, as a permanent memory to his life in Granada, where he composed a great deal of his work.

Several circumstances enabled us to carry out this idea; all of Manuel's furniture and belongings had been carefully stored by his friends in Granada since his house was closed in 1941 by María Paula Montes de Borrajo, following my uncle's instructions. Thanks to the delightful drawings, reproduced in this book, of every corner of the house, done by his dear friend and distinguished artist, Hermenegildo Lanz, everything has been faithfully reconstructed.

We were fortunate in receiving the enthusiastic support of Manuel Sola Rodríguez-Bolívar, at that time Mayor of Granada, and in 1962 his Town Council purchased the property to become, later, the house and museum of Manuel de Falla.

After the purchase of the house by the Town Council, and the donation of the furniture by Falla's family, the next step to be taken was a more delictate one, the restoration and installation of the House. In this respect we are very grateful for the dedicated collaboration of Manuel Orozco Diaz, who directed the authentic restoration of the charming but simple little hou-

se where my uncle and my Aunt María del Carmen lived, and which is now a delightful, nostalgic corner in memory of the composer who spent the best years of his life in Granada, as well as composing much of his best work here.

24th December, 1968.

Manuel de Falla's House

*Today has been beautiful
and Granada was wonderful.*

Manuel de Falla's House

Manuel Orozco

In the summer of 1921 Manuel de Falla rented this house, which became his established home in Granada, although he had lived in the city since the previous year. Falla was then 45, and had composed a considerable part of his work, and in Granada he was to compose the second part of his work, the purist and most internationally known of his music: Master Peter's Puppet Show, the Harpsichord Concerto, Psyche, Sonnet to Córdoba, Tribute to Dukas, to Debussy, to Arbós and to Pedrell, and almost the entire Atlántida, which took up twenty years of his life. Working together with Federico García Lorca, he wrote the scores for the Mystery Plays of Calderón, the poet's puppet plays, and participated in the Cante Jondo competitions. Undoubtedly Falla spent some of his calmest, though most painful years, here in Granada.

Since his arrival in Granada in 1919 "to work in peace", until 1921, Falla lived in the Carmen of Santa Engracia, No. 43, Real de la Alhambra, now demolished. This, his first home in Granada, was the property of Antonio Barrios "el Polinario", the father of his friend Angel. When his parents died in July of 1919, he brought some of their furniture to this house, at the same time as ordering some of his own to be made.

Adolfo Salazar visited Falla after the first night of the Tricorne, and commented: "After wandering up through the wonderful gardens and the impressive Gate of Justice, the finely balanced proportions of the Gate of Wine evoke the emotional memory of the «prelude», in which the French genius sang about it, visualizing it in his imagination"[1].

A little further up, and at the end of a row of houses gathered on the top of the Alhambra hill, we find Manuel de Falla's rustic retreat, the brilliance of white-washed walls broken by the blue door and windows. The interior is of the utmost simplicity, and quiet, good taste, with a hint of influence of Zuloaga, for instance in the rush half —panell ing on the walls, held in place with huge old nails, against which the blue of the furniture stood out remarkably.

According to Salazar, the room was tinged with an orange light filtering through the striped, Alpujarra curtains[2]; and a big porcelain jug gleamed in one corner. Ripe quinces and pomegranates blocked out the distant silhouete of the Sierra Nevada, and the cypresses of the Generalife could barely be discerned through the intertwined jazmin. The heavy heat of October seems bearable under the dense roof of creeping vines, with the accompaniment of a nearby, murmuring fountain. This seems almost poetic, maestro, doesn't it? Falla

smiles and half closes his eyes. Throughout those long years in Paris Falla's ilusion was to live in Granada; now he seemed to be living in a dream world. There are a thousand different images of the Sierra Nevada, the fertile valley which seems to disappear into the horizon, like an imaginary seat at dusk, reflecting a myriad of stars in its shining surface, and they create a sense of peace and calm, engulfing his mind and spirit".

The hard winters of Granada and the north winds which whistled down this particular street, together with the delicate state of his lungs, forced Falla to a move the following year.

In 1920, quite decided on living in Granada, Falla wrote to Angel Barrios, asking him to find him "a little house and garden with good views. Possibilities: Alhambra, Carrera del Darro or Vistillas." Having spent a year in the house in Real Street, he now found that the one in Antequerela Alta fulfilled almost all his desires. Situated on the southern hill of the Alhambra, the street called Antequerela or Caidero owes its name, as tradition goes, to the Moors who fled from the Christian re-occupation of Antequera in 1410, or from the name of Caidero as a derivation from the Arabic word cadí (mayor), home or residence of the mayor.

During the Middle Ages in Granada this was a quiet and sunny district, where both gentry and artesans lived side by side, almost as nowadays. In fact the carmen (as Alhambra houses are called) "Ave Maria", number 11 on the hill, was first a workshop for weaving and dye-ing and up until the XIXth century for silk-weaving, lace-making and dye-ing, all crafts very much to Muslim tastes, which must have reached their peak during the centuries of the Arab Kingdom of Granada.

This minute house, together with Nos. 7 and 9, belonged to the Pineda López family, relations of Mariana Pineda, the heroine of freedom, and later they were passed on to their descendants, the Arroyo family, from whom the City Council bought the property in 1962.

Traditional Granada silk-making was still being continued at the time of the Pinedas in these little houses. Several families of artesans lived in them, one of which, the Moras, worked in both silk and lace. Another family, the Abrils, also lived in the same house, which acquired certain fame; one of the sons stabbed and killed his own father, and afterwards took refuge in a cellar under the house where he was found and taken away to be hung. There was a lingering superstition about the house on account of the gruesome drama which had taken place there. Falla, however, found it a very quiet and peaceful place, perfectly adecuate for his composing.

His friends, Federico, Fernando Vilches, Cerón, Manuel Angeles Ortiz; González Méndez and Torres Balbás, helped with the move across the Alhambra walks. In his letters Falla wrote"... The house of the Mártires and this low sky are wonderful". "You undoubtedly need to come and live in Villa del Oso as much as I do in Antequeruela Alta, where I have the most beautiful panoramic view in the world... You can see that I have already become a complete "Granadino". From now onwards Falla would head his letters "Beautiful Granada", "The Antequerela", and to Trend he wrote: "Come to Granada! How glad I would be, there is a wonderful autumn climate!"

Falla carried out some building altera-
tiones to the house, made an inside stair-
case, and bought some typical locally made furniture. Legendre visited him in this
house in 1922, and commented: ''About
midday on 13th June, I was going up the
Alhambra Hill, and I knocked on the door
of the house where Falla lived. From Antequerela Alta the whole of the fertile valley of Granada could be overlooked, and
it seemed as though the crystalline, pure
light from the peaks of the Sierra Nevada
enhanced the deep green-ness of the plain,
at the same time leaving a light mist over
the distant horizon.

''The maid eased the door ajar, and I
let myself into a darkened room. My eyes
gradually became accustomed to the semi-
darkness and I was able to distinguish a
multitude of flowers in each corner, filling
the atmosphere with their fragrance. The
composer walked in and stood there, lit by
a beam of sunlight; he was a man of me-
dium height, whose large, deep, shining
eyes were the outstanding feature in his
clean-shaven face; a finely-shaped forehead
rose above his eyes, but the lower half of
his face had more severe features, distinctly
outlined, though often melting away into

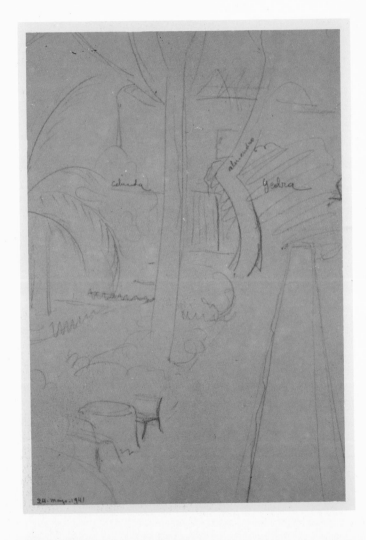

one of his infinitely kind smiles. Falla invited me into the sunlit room where he worked''.

Several years later García Gómez described his house for us: ''Share with me my memories of Antequerela Alta, his home in Granada before that final journey. The house seems to be hidden in a quiet corner, while overlooking a myriad of lights across the Valley of Granada. It is decorated with pot plants, lovingly tended by Manuel's sister, Maria del Carmen. A low little room opens out to the right of the door, with local rush matting and wrought-iron work. There is a statue of the Virgen by Murillo[3], which seems to be smiling at the modern painting on the opposite wall. Everything is spotlessly clean, (upstairs too: the piano, the gramophone, the books, are all spotlessly clean). Around the round table with its typical ground-length cloth there are rush-seated chairs where some friends are conversing with Falla. One of Maria del Carmen's cats is purring in one corner. The composer lights a cigarette, having first used and ivory toothpick to push in a small piece of cotton wool as a filter, and he seems to be counting the puffs. The conversation is about everything other than

music. Falla enquires, listens, and invariably amazes us with his exquisitely polite commentaries''.

This, then, was Manuel de Falla's house which they saw, and which remained intact when on 28th September, 1939, the door was closed on a significant period of his life, leaving behind some of his most prized possessions, books, scores, and of course, memories. ''Remember to look after my piano and keep it tuned'', he said to his friend, Pedro Ghys[4]. As from that day it was to be María Paula Montes de Borrajo who acted as the devoted custodian of the musician's house.

Everything in Falla's house remained intact under the vigilance of María Paula, who sometimes received orders to send on books or scores, until 1941, when some silver cutlery was stolen by burglars who abounded in that area. Falla then decided to dismantle the house and put the furniture into store. On 27th January he wrote from Villa del Lago to his friends: ''My dear Pedro and María Paula, we were very pleased to hear your news at Christmas and the New Year. God willing, my health, and world affairs, will allow us to meet again soon.

''María del Carmen is writing to you with our ideas concerning the house since it was broken into. We suppose that the burglars in questions have by now been set free. That is our wish, and I beg you to communicate our desire to the appropriate authorities''.

Among other things, María del Carmen said: ''As our return still seems to be distant, unfortunately, we continue to think about our house, ''Huerta Chica'' back in Córdoba[5]. We think it would be most practical to leave the house in Antequerela, and store everything in complete safety. I would be grateful if you would take the piano into your house. The books should be cleaned one by one (with great care, as Manolo prizes them so)''.

On hearing Falla's decision, Hermenegildo Lanz tried to dissuade him, as his friends would miss this delightful corner. But Falla was adamant in his decision.

Our close friend Hermenegildo Lanz, to whom we are so deeply indebted, confronted by Falla's determination, asked the composer's permission to make some diagrams and drawings which would de invaluable to re-install the furniture in the

event of his friend's return. His drawings constitute the first step towards the preservation of the composer's house.

María Paula Montes de Borrajo, following Falla's instructions, had the house carefully and lovingly packed up. This was a thankless task, in which she even went to the extent of adding a page to the thousands of books, giving their section, bookcase and position. Absolutely everything belonging to Falla and his sister was packed up in 1941, and kept in the Granada convent of Santa Inés, where Valentín Ruiz Aznar, friend of the composer, was chaplain. When this religious order closed and was transferred to the Convent of Los Angeles, Falla's furniture remained in the Convent of Santa Inés, and was later moved to Valentín's own family home, where it remained until 1962.

A group of Falla's friends, among us Professor Luis Jiménez, and the pianist García Carrillo, tried to rent the house, once it was empty, as a meeting-place for music-lovers. However, the owner, Sr. Porras, made it clear that he was unwilling to rent it while Don Manuel still lived. A similar effort by the Town Council proved

to be in vain too, and the carmen remained closed, and inevitably somewhat forgotten by the people of Granada.

In 1943, three years before Falla's death, Manuel de Falla's house was let to the Duchess of Lécera. On a visit to this delightful lady, at the same time a close friend, we expressed our wish that the home of our "Granada" composer should be preserved as much as possible. The new occupant was appreciative of our wishes, and her immense charm, personality and social distinction converted the garden into a rendezvous for some of the outstanding musical and artistic personalities of the time. We are extremely grateful for the interest taken by this distinguished friend.

Of course, the Duchess carried out certain alterations and improvements in the house and garden, the boundary walls, and changed some floor-tiling, windows, and the kitchen.

In 1962, the Town Council decided to expropriate the property. It was the Mayor at that time, Manuel Sola Rodríguez Bolívar who dealt personally with the composer's beneficiaries, María del Carmen, his sister, and María Isabel de Falla, daughter

of Germán who died in 1959, both of whom generously donated everything in the Granada house to the city for it to be restored and opened to the public; this proposal has been carried out by the city corporation.

So the organization for the opening of the house was set up, and after the death of the Duchess of Lécera in 1963 the process of re-installing Falla's house began.

With the advice of María Paula Montes, written descriptions, photographs and sketches by Lanz, almost everything, even the most seemingly insignificant object, was placed just as it has been in the composer's lifetime.

Manuel de Falla's house had been fated to remain empty of his furniture for more than two decades. Fate also willed the incomparable generosity of María del Carmen Falla and Maribel in donating this treasure, and it is to them Granada owes this invaluable spiritual retreat.

Falla's furniture and personal belongings have been arranged in the different rooms, garden and patio, strictly in accordance with written documents. It was

hardly advisable to follow the verbal descriptions of those who visited the house in the past, as Falla himself frecuently made changes in the position of his furniture, particularly his piano and work bureau, at different times of the year. Photographs of the composer in his house show the changes he made in its position.

We have placed the pictures and furniture as Falla had them in 1939 when he left his house, coinciding with the drawings made by Lanz for that very purpose, and which are a visual proof of their position. In the patio and garden as well as in the rooms, Hermenegildo Lanz drew everything with great accuracy. Only in certain cases where there is irrevocable evidence of photographs, which we have also used in other publications[6], and where Falla can be seen with his furniture, have we respected these positions rather than those in the drawings by Lanz; although they were done at a later date, they necessarily had to give way to the more graphic evidence of photographs.

With respect to the floor-tiling and some windows, we have been obliged to accept the changes of the next tenant, among

other reasons because of the fact that during Falla's occupancy neither his financial state nor his particular demands for comfort called for, or permitted, any unecessary improvements. The tiles in both the study and dining-room were therefore changed, as explained, and in our opinion the clay tiling is in fact more in fitting with the furnishing and decoration than the old flagstones shown in the 1932 photographs and removed in 1945.

Manuel de Falla's house is, therefore, the most authentic record of the life of the composer at the height of his career, and the only home he left behind when he set out for the Argentine, taking only his work on Atlántida and the minimum of clothes, leaving all the rest of his personal belongings here, where they still remain. All the general house and kitchen ware, his scores and contents of the library, were also left in the Granada house.

It has been considered unwise to leave the thousands of books and scores in the present house, as this would require specific safety precautions, as at present the house is inadequately prepared for such valuable contents, and the simplicity of it

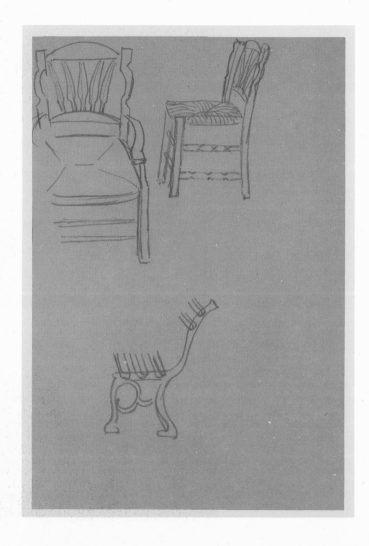

might be spoilt if these measures were taken. The ideal plan is for the entirety of the works from Falla's house to be installed in a nearby building where they can be adequately safeguarded and used for reference by scholars.

This simple little house is the dearest and most genuine tribute to Manuel de Falla, a living memory to a worldwide composer who chose to live and compose in Granada. The city is infinitely indebted to him, because in one way or another it is ever present in his music; as early as the Vida Breve (Short Life), composed even before he came to Granada, until the composition of Atlántida, shows his devotion to the city, and to a certain extent everything he composed is a reflection of the closeness and faithfulness he felt for his beloved city.

His sister, María del Carmen, came to live in the house years after his death. She spent part of 1966, 67, 68 living there; the addition of some stoves and other improvements had been made since she left it in 1939. A renewed life was given to the house with the stay of this elderly lady, erstwhile beloved and faithful companion of the composer.

Man leaves traces behind him; an intangible sense of his presence pervades the objects which were impregnated by him, and something remains of the spirit and being of the person who shared the same existence, and who left there signs of his trembling pulse and beating heart. This little house miraculously retains something of the spirit and intangible presence of this exceptional man and artist.

Let this quiet, peaceful and venerable retreat be Granada's literary and historical heritage to the world, and to those who are in search of the spirit of one of the most exceptional, unsophisticated yet brilliant men of our age.

FOOTNOTES

1. Debussy used a postcard sent by Falla of the Gate of Wine in the Alhambra, as an inspiration for the work of the same title. He received numerous postcards of the buildings, especially of the Arab Palace, which the composer used as themes for his compositions. Hence Arabesques, Claire de Lune, etc.

2. Salazar refers to some weavings from the Alpujarras, and to a straw-type curtain which Falla used in that window. Adalfo Salazar. Symphony and Ballet. Mundo Latino. Madrid.

3. García Gómez, La Silla del Moro and Nuevas Escenas Andaluzas, Colección Austral, Espasa Calpe. Attributed to Murillo, not confirmed at a later date.

4. Sr. Ghys, friend and neighbour of Falla, restored the XVI th century organ of Saint Cecilia, the composer's parish church. This organ, which gave its name to the adjacent area of the Realejo, was a beautiful instrument, first restored by him, and frecuently played by him too. After 1939, under later parish priests, it fell into disrepair; it may be that it was valuable, even after being taken apart and sold. Pedro Ghys, a Granadino of Belgian origen, tuned Falla's piano up until his death.

5. In this letter María del Carmen is referring to Córdoba in Spain, and calling it "ours", as she had known it when they were in search of silence and of a hideaway, at a time when the noises of war allowed them no peace in which to work or rest.

6. Manuel Orozco - Falla. Publisher: Destino, Barcelona 1968. "Heroes of History". Biography of Manuel de Falla. Publisher: Codex, Madrid.

Manuel de Falla

... With the only compensation of seeing the mountains covered in snow. Fantastic! this is what was missing the other morning in the "Carmen de los Mártires".

Manuel de Falla

Enrique Franco

 It is my wish that this short biography should be consistent with Falla's demands. With regard to the contents, I have paid greater attention to his work than to him as a person, as Manuel would have liked. Its presentation is neat, brief and straightforward, in other words, it fulfils the objective which the composer desired for all music.

While working on other essays on Falla, and at the same time trying to complete the important volume which I began several years ago, I am also hopeful that this present publication may achieve a reasonable circulation, without my having, of course, any great literary aspirations; there can be nothing further from the mind of the person concerned than such a highly presumptuous style, written with the best of intentions, but in fact proving to be somewhat contemptuous towards the readers.

We have reason enough to believe that music-lovers in Spain have outgrown such intellectual problems, and they no longer need to resort to anecdotes, intense patriotism or an otherwise picturesque approach. It is my hope that these modest and truthful pages may prove useful.

I. 1876

When Falla was born in a flat in number 3, Mina Square, Cadiz, Spain had just embarked on the restoration period. In the heart of our society there were the first signs of tenseness, which were to grow beyond control. Let us remember that in that same year, 1876, Giner de los Ríos founded the Institute of Free Teaching, while Menéndez Pelayo began his great controversy over "Science in Spain" with the followers of Kraus. In the literary world, Galdós published "Doña Perfecta", Pereida his "Outlines in tempera". The unsure bourgeois society found enjoyment in "Festival Poems" by Eusebio Blasco, now forgotten, and in the opera, Spanish light opera and bull-fighting.

A storm of controversy arose over the Theatre Royal production of Wagner's "Rienzi", because the public were faithful lovers of Italian opera and were more receptive to Meyerber's "Star of the North", Auber's "Fra Diavolo", or Thomas' "Mignon". A few even ventured the production of some Spanish opera: Chapí first with "The Ships of Cortés" and "Garcilaso", and then "Jefte's daughter"; other lyrical composers vied with Chapí, but other than Bretón, the rest have faded into relative oblivion: Reparaz, Fernández Grajal, Aceves, Emilio Serrano, Casamitjana, Pinilla and Carreras. In 1874 Felipe Pedrell gave the first performance of "L'ultimo Abenzeraggio" and "Quasimodo". Three composer-performers spread Spanish music abroad: the guitarist Tárraga, the violinist Sarasate and the tenor Gayarre. In the samey year as Falla, another of the great "universal" Spaniards was born in Vendrell, Pablo Casals, the 'cellist. One year before Ravel was born, and one year after,

Wanda Landowska, both of whom were very significant in Falla's life.

The highlight of European music in 1976 was the opening of the Bayreuth theatre with Wagner's "Ring of the Nibelungs". A year earlier Bizet's Carmen had impressed Europe with Spain's musical personality and atmosphere, previously hinted at by Merimée; also a season before, Moussorgsky's "Boris Godunov" taught what a popular national opera could be. Other events hailed the eve of modern times: Otto constructed the "piston engine" and Bell invented the telephone. Mallarmé's poem written the year of Falla's birth was not of lesser significance; "L'après-midi d'un faune" was the inspiration that served as a spark to Claude Debussy's impressionist revolution.

Apart from several isolated XVIIIth and XIXth century composers, the world of Spanish music had undergone a particularly lethargic period, mainly as a result of the enormous influence of Italian opera on the court. Therefore, at the end of XIXth century Spain was, musically speaking, quite insignificant. Maybe we were just of picturesque interest, particularly to the romantics of the time, who saw only a superficial reflection of Andalusian characteristics, without probing any deeper into the music of the south.

In his essay on his maestro, Felipe Pedrell, Falla laments this sad situation: ''It is not my intention to deny that some of the works of our XIXth century composers are worthy of considerable respect and even admiration. These composers are outstanding in one respect, light opera. However, this mixture of light-hearted Spanish song and Italian opera constituted an artistic production for a Spanish audience only, and for a limited audience too. Such works, almost always too hastily composed and with insufficient musical technique, were generally-speaking of minor musical importance. The main aim of the composers was far from being artistic, it was just to stage and perform their productions as soon as possible. Some composers of opera or even sacred music did attempt to reach higher musical standards, but with a few notable exceptions, they achieved no more than a poor imitation of the Italian operas, and this marked the beginning of a period of decadence of a great musical nation''.

II. FROM CADIZ TO MADRID

Such was the cultural environment in 1876, the date of Manuel de Falla's birth in Cádiz, a city of great political and intellectual tradition, Spain's balcony over the Atlantic, and sometimes called the ''first Latin-American city''. Falla's first contact with music was through ''La Morilla'', one of the household maids of Moorish descent, who recounted him some of the old ballads, enlivened with songs and dances, which gave free rein to the imagination of ''Manolito'', who had always been such an introverted little boy. From his mother and his music teacher, Eloísa Galluzo, he learnt his first steps in music, and he himself confessed he was first inspired to take up music as a result of the concerts he attended in Cádiz Museum, against the setting of some of Zurbaran's magnificent paintings.

With the aim of perfecting his piano studies, Falla visited Madrid frecuently, to attend classes given by one of the best teachers of the time, José Tragó. He decided to settle in Madrid permanently, but before doing so he had already outlined some of his first compositions, among them some for 'cello and piano, dedicated to Sal-

vador Viniegra, and these could be considered "Opus 1" of Falla's preliminary period. In 1899 the future composer won the
first prize for piano in Madrid's Royal
Conservatory.

Falla needed to expand and make a name for himself, among other reasons to sol-
ve his financial problems, in order to continue with his musical studies, first of all
in Madrid, and later abroad. He had no
choice other than to cater for the musical
taste of the moment, light opera. Between
1900 and 1903 Falla composed five light
operas: Limosna de amor, El corneta de órdenes, La cruz de Malta (the latter two together with Amadeo Vives, one of the
"well-known" composers of the time), La
Casa de Tócame Roque, based on a one-
act farce by Ramón de la Cruz, and Los
amores de la Inés. The latter was the only
one which was received with a certain de-
gree of success in the Comedy Theatre, and
La casa de Tócame Roque was the only light
opera Falla had any respect for, in fact he
went so far as to use some ideas from it in
El sombrero de tres picos (The Three-
cornered hat), the ballet designed for
Diaghilev.

Several events were undoubtedly important in Falla's life. His name achieved certain popularity through a song, Tus ojillos
negros (Your little black eyes), written by
him in 1902, based on the poem of a little-
known poet, Cristobal de Castro, and
which became extrordinarily successful,
and which even now is quite frequently
sung. Although it is hardly representative
of Falla's style, there are traces of the composer's future personality. Of far greater
significance was his introduction to Felipe
Pedrell, of whom Falla immediately wanted to become a follower, and to whom he
confessed he owed his artistic career, and
that initiation which is essential to a willing and well-meaning beginner.

III. "THE BRIEF LIFE"

Felipe Pedrell was a kind of apostle, mi-
sunderstood in his lifetime, who made a
dual effort to raise the standards of our
music, presenting the best of forgotten
music from our past, and anticipating a
reawaken-ing of Spanish music based on
its nationalist differences. (Pedrell published organ and polyphony anthologies by
Spanish composers, and a collection of a

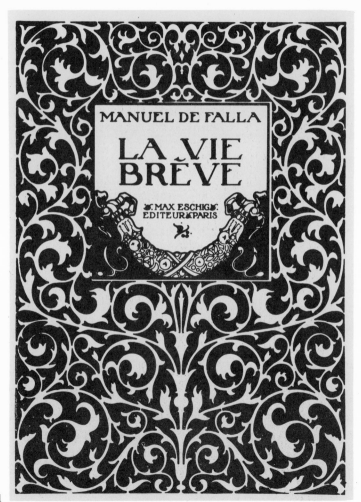

MANUEL DE FALLA

LA VIE
BRÊVE

MAX ESCHIG
EDITEUR PARIS

1

2

range of popular music). The important thing about Pedrell's attitude is not his merely popular nationalism, but the historicist aspect, which led him to make detailed studies into the features which define the very essence of the Spanish character in both the works of great composers of the past and in "natural" music. If in his work Pedrell did not in fact achieve his aim, at least he pointed the way to others to do so. Pedrell has therefore been justifiably referred to as protagonist of our "modern musical renaissance". He was the source of inspiration to the great trilogy. Albéniz, Granados and Falla, who gave renewed confidence as well as a personality of its own to Spanish music on a worldwide basis.

In 1905 and 1906 two events of major importance were to occur, which had resounding significance in Falla's aesthetic outlook and the development of his musical career; he won first prize in the Academia de Bellas Artes competition for a one-act opera, with "the brief life", with Carlos Fernández-Shaw's libretto; then, Falla found in the Madrid Book Fair a small book by Louis Lucas, published in 1849 in Paris, called Acoustique Nouvelle. While Pedrell's writings and compositions confirmed some of Falla's intuitions, this modest book by an almost unknown essayist offered him the systematized principles which were to predominate in his harmonic system, based on the play of naturally resonant sounds, closely linked to melody, rhythm and tone. These were principles which Falla had studied in the natural harmonic possibilities of the guitar —which so aroused Debussy's interest— and in the works of Domenich Scarlatti, the internal structure of which were to have such a marked influence on our composer's work, as had the musical expression in his compositions.

"The Brief Life" has been misinterpreted by critics, reviewers and even by performers[1]; some have said that it derives from light opera, and others that it merely originates from the most popular aspects of ballads or folk dances. In reality, though, "The Brief Life" is an intense musical drama, in which the musical and dramatical elements are perfectly welded together. Falla soon displays an "imaginary foklorism" in his opera, an epithet which was only applied much later in Bartok's creative period. The only direct reference to folklore in "The Brief Life" is in the second dance. The rest is pure invention derived from certain characteristics of Andalusian musical language, elements which make up the style of the music and which Falla incorporates into the overall development of greater importance. The one-act opera must be understood and interpreted in this context, and with out overemphasizing that reference to folklore. The harmony and melody as well as the orchestration are purely Falla's own style, and in essence they are evident throughout all his works, although at a later stage he tends towards more "economical" means, to broader outlines. However, the Andalusian element is not a fundamental part of the score, though it may be the most easily recognizable. His "manner", in the future applied to aims far from being Andalusian, is what dominates and signifies the great discovery before Falla's departure from Spain and his contact with other circles. So much so that the score of "The Brief Life" was to open the doors to Parisian circles, to the friendship of and discipleship to Paul Dukas, who listened to the whole of the composition, and afterwards remarked "This must be performed in the "Opera Comique".

IV. PARIS

When Falla was able to raise the necessary money, mainly thanks to several concerts, he fulfilled his coveted aim of going to Paris. He arrived in the French capital at the beginning of the summer of 1907. His first job was as a pianist and conductor, and instead of playing concert music, Falla's job was to accompany a miming company on a "tournée" through the Vosges, in the north of France and Switzerland. These new contacts proved to be very encouraging to the composer, although the remuneration was hardly plentiful. On his return to Paris he established contact with Dukas, who agreed to be his musical adviser; immediately afterwards he introduced him to Isaac Albéniz, and later to Debussy, Ricardo Viñes, Mauricio Ravel, Satie and Stravinsky.

Dukas, Debussy and Ravel were precisely the friends who managed to persuade Durand to publish "Piezas Españolas", which Falla had already drafted before leaving Spain. They are dedicated to Isaac Albéniz, but they were not, as is sometimes thought, inspired by "Iberia" by Albeniz, although there are certain similarities with reference to typical characteristics of popular Spanish expressions. Falla's compositions for piano are, however, much clearer and sharper, far from the baroque style of Albeniz's last period, moreover, the composer himself admitted having written his works without any concern for the actual instruments; this was something to which he gave priority later in his "Fantasía Bética". His four themes, Aragonesa, Cubana, Montañesa and Andaluza are quite different from the structure of those by Albeniz. Here we find Falla's characteristic method, carried out to perfection in Aragonesa, that is, a whole folio is elaborated from the essence of just one brief theme, to such an extent that it is to be found in the two introductory bars. That is the essence of the whole piece, and other elements that appear can be interpreted as multiple variations on the theme. We can also recall Noches and Concerto, in both of which the first movement is based on one theme only; in Generalife this theme appears at the beginning, but in the case of Concerto it is to be found half-way through the movement, and therefore the development takes place before the actual introduction of the main theme, or from

another point of view, the variations are leading up to a natural culminating point, the theme. On the other hand, Montañesa, which has a subtitle, Paisaje, is the most rhapsodic of the pieces in which the composer uses a more direct, popular style.

Falla wished to pay due respect to what he considered his "second mother country", and he was equally anxious to put words to music, not only in his mother tongue, but also in other languages, in an effort to master the difficulties of converting words into music. In 1909 he complete Trois Mélodies, based on Théophile Gautier's verses, Les Colombes, Chinoiserie and Seguidille; the latter is a translation of a Spanish poem by Bretón de los Herreros. A certain exotic vein dominates these songs, even regarding what is Spanish from a foreign point of view; these songs so enchanted Claude Debussy, perhaps because they combine two of his most favourite themes, Spain and the Orient.

Manuel de Falla's seven years in Paris, from 1907-1914, proved to be one of the most fruitful periods in his life, and with few exceptions, his health was not affected, as was to happen later on, prolonging interminably his work on Atlántida. As well as perfecting La Vida Breve for its first performance in Nice and Paris, for which he made certain modifications in the score, he also composed "Nocturnes for piano and orchestra, and "Siete Canciones Populares" (Seven Popular Songs). The latter two works constitute two closely related, but different ways of setting out the problem of "foklorism".

When composing his Canciones, the composer turned to the roots of tradition, even though it may be somewhat exaggerated to refer to simple "harmonies" Don Manuel selected seven melodies from "Cancioneros" by Pedrell, Ocón, Inzenga, Hernández and others. In some cases he respected the original form as in "Paño", "Asturiana" or "Seguidilla"; in others, such as "Nana" and "Canción" he makes considerable changes, and in yet others, "Jota" and "Polo", there is as much personal invention as there is original matter. But what gives the touch of genius to it as a whole is the achievement of Pedrell's theory: the harmonic extraction of the melodic features of each song. Falla builds on this concept and transfers it into music in a piano score of such perfection that voice and piano merge in complete unison. His search for variety lead the composer never to repeat a theme with the same harmony, and the synthesis of elements which make up "Canciones" constitute the clearest explanation of Falla's method, which he heard Pedrell expound, which he always felt in his inner self, and which he studied and analysed in Lucas' "Acoustique Nouvelle".

V. EL AMOR BRUJO

If we extend the concepts we have explained for the Spanish compositions and the folk song, and we blend together the combination of piano-orchestra, or rather orchestra with piano, (Falla wished the soloist in his "Nocturnos" to sit among the ensemble), then we have the interpretation of "Noches en los Jardines de España" (Nights in the gardens of Spain). To these possibilities we add another, that of a colourful and always "resonant" orchestra. A fine attainment of his "imaginary folkorism" (according to Falla there is only one reference to folklore, in a minor chord at the beginning), the intention of "Nocturnos" is to a certain extent, and in spite of the obvious impressionist influence, different to that of Debussy. The author of "Pelleas" only seeks to "suggest", while that of "Nights" is admirable. We have already mentioned the first "nocturno"; as much could be said about the third, whose "verse", with such an outstanding personality, is repeated time and again and is the basic theme of the whole movement. Even the strength of the base notes on the piano with a theme reminiscent of the "zorongo" is a variant on a previous orchestral theme. This series of derivations and relations serves to strengthen the texture, just as a performer who understands it distinctly will make a grave mistake by interpreting "Nights" with a rhapsodic style which is far from the composer's intention.

"Nights in the Gardens of Spain", to which Falla devoted so much time in Paris, had to be finished in Spain; the First World War obliged Don Manuel to return. Madrid paid due tribute to the composer in a ceremony at the Ateneo, in honour of both Falla and Turina, who had also just returned from the French capital. And that was not all. "La Vida Breve", already performed in Nice and Paris, was finally performed at the Zarzuela Theatre, the rôle of "Salud" sung by the soprano Luisa Vela, who had also taken part in the "Seven Popular Songs" at the Ateneo.

Falla still had not tired of the Andalusian themes, nor were the Madrid critics going to ask more of him. Therefore, when the comedy writer, Gregorio Martínez Sierra, who was very much in vogue at the time, communicated to him Pastora Imperio's wish for him to write something on a gipsy theme, he did not hesitate to accept. It is difficult to be precise about the origins of "El amor brujo". The idea was to stage certain gipsy traditions, legends and rites which Falla learnt first hand from Pastora Imperio herself, just as previously he had heard the true "jondo" singing from Pastora's mother, Rosario "La Mejorana". There followed a series of songs, dances and dialogues, all fairly brief, accompanied by a small orchestral group. Falla must have felt the music "El amor brujo" deep down in his soul, for he completed the whole piece in five months. The first night was on 15th April, 1915 in the Lara Theatre, Madrid, and it was received with mixed response. This was hardly surprising, considering the originality of "El amor brujo'' and the type of Andalusian concepts to which the audiences and critics were accustomed. Nevertheless, this piece on the gipsy way of life was to be one of Falla's most popular works. After its first performance he revised it, expanded the original chamber scoring and eliminated the dialogue, converting it into a ballet. Although there is no actual quotation of folk melodies, it is a remarkable distillation of Andalusian folk music, ''jondo'', a true reflection of its deep feelings and emotions; the same feelings were later to be expressed by Federico García Lorca in his ''Romancero Gitano''. As a ballet, in which Antonia Marcé, ''La Argentina'' had such a resounding success, and as an orchestral suite, ''El amor brujo'' has always been one of the most outstanding examples of Manuel de Falla's creative talent.

VI. EL SOMBRERO DE TRES PICOS (THE THREE-CORNERED HAT)

The great talent, Serge Diaghilev, was interested in Falla's Music and had planned a ballet based on ''Nights in the Gardens of Spain''. But for some time the composer had been considering the idea of staging, either as opera or ballet, Pedro Antonio de Alarcón's novel based on the ancient ballad ''The three-cornered hat'', or ''También la corregidora guapa'' (the Chief Magistrate's beautiful wife). He set to work on his proposal, but the difficulties caused by the First World War meant a considerable modification, and as a mime version of the folk tale ''El corregidor y la molinera'' was given its first performance in Madrid in 1917. Diaghilev was present, and realized that once suitably reshaped and rescored, with ''El sombrero de Tres Picos'' he could add Manuel de Falla's name to his important repertoire of ballets.

There is an important difference between the two parts of ''El sombrero de tres picos'', a disproportionate use of the instruments; the first part is still scored as for the mimed version of ''El corregidor..'', for a small orchestra, while the second part is composed for a full symphony orchestra. The ballet based on Alarcón's novel is an impressive one, with several characteristics to be mentioned; the style is more in tone with other successful contemporary composers in Europe, particularly Stravinsky;

3

4

there is a more abundant reference to folk melodies[2]; many of the themes are well-known and still survive; for example, "Canción de la novia", basis for the dance "Danza de Vecinos"; "Canción de Granada", which is also introduced in "Seven Popular songs", and which is used for the grapes scene; "El Paño", used in some songs, and various other themes, popular, guitar or for children. There are some fascinating orchestral effects which evoke both the plucking and strumming sounds of the guitar. It is interesting to observe that in "Le Tricorne" for the first time we can distinguish the "neoscarlattian" expressions, which Falla was also to used in the "Retablo" and the "Concerto" and which were to become a predominant theme among composers of the following generation: the Halffters, Rodrigo, Bautista. When neoclassicism was at its culminating moment, Spanish composers recurred to Domenich Scarlatti, who Falla considered to be as Spanish as the other great Domenich, not born in Spain, but owing so much to the country; I am referring to El Greco. Diaghilev's first performance of "El sombrero de Tres Picos", with choreography by Massine and settings by Pablo Picasso, was held in the Alhambra Theatre, in London, on 22nd July, 1919.

VII. FUEGO FATUO

It was 1918, and Manuel de Falla, together with some of his erstwhile companions, Gregorio and María Martínez Sierra, decided to write a comic opera based on some of Chopin's themes; Chopin was a composer whose music Falla had constantly admired since the days of his piano career. It was by no means about the whole life of the Polish composer as is often mistakenly believed; it dealt with an amorous conflict which can be summarized as follows: two women vied for the love of one man; one symbolized an angel, i.e. goodness, gentleness and honesty, while the other was an example of unbridled passion. According to María Martínez Sierra, virtually sole author of the libretto, this conflict was singularly distasteful to Falla.

Don Manuel worked unceasingly on the elaboration, not just the orchestration, of Chopin themes, for which the librettist adapted the text of the songs. Gregorio Martínez Sierra used all his influence in the dramatic world to guarantee a first performance in least possible time, in the Esclave Theatre, then under the management of the well-known theatrical composer, Manuel Penella, as Falla was loath to dedicate himself fully to the task without the assurance that the work would be staged immediately. He had the bitter memory of ''La Vida Breve'', awarded a prize in Madrid in 1905, staged in Nice in 1913, in Paris in 1914, and only finally performed in Madrid's Zarzuela Theatre in the same year.

The copyists of the Sociedad de Autores (Writers' Society) were reproducing the originals handed in by Falla, and Don Manuel Fontanals, the costume designer, had all the designs prepared. However, there were delays over the first, performance, because of the singer, Aga Lahovska, who wanted it staged in Barcelona, and then the conductor of the Comic Opera of Paris, Carré, turned down the offer, because, in his own words, ''he wanted music by Falla and not by Chopin''. The fact is that when the draft of three acts was completed, and only the first and third had been set to music, Don Manuel condemned the ''Fuego Fatuo'' to his archives and banished it from his mind.

Could it be that Don Manuel found the libretto distasteful, as the author, María Martínez Sierra, hints at in her memoirs? Perhaps Falla reflected on the advisability, then considerable and nowadays complete, of adapting Chopin's piano music into arias, duos and concertos. Whatever the reason, we are totally unaware of it. On the other hand, there is no doubt that the composer had a high opinion of his work. This is evident from the fact that Falla constantly included it in the catalogue of his works, frequently requested for biographies, encyclopaedias or articles.

When I was entrusted with the organization of Falla's archives by his heirs Isabel de Falla and her husband the arquitect, García de Paredes, and I found the original completed two acts of ''Fuego Fatuo'', it occurred to me that because of the originality and brilliance of the work based on Chopin, it might be worth hearing. However, it seemed unfeasible, or even inadvisable to complete the score and perform it half a century after its commencement. His heirs were in agreement with me, as were other authorities (conductors, composers and musicologists), whom I consulted on the matter.

Therefore there was only one solution, to convert Falla's music into an instrumental "suite", suitable to be played at a concert, or even to adapt it as a ballet, which will surely not be delayed. Nor do I know of any other orchestral version of Chopin which is so perfectly composed, and with such exquisite harmonic arrangements, often quite distinct from the original. By means of clarity of the sound texture, and the magnificent choral arrangement, Falla evokes Chopin through his own music. Definitively, he later did the same in "Pedrelliana", using extracts from "La Celestina", although in this case Don Manuel's work was produced to greater perfection, rather than from inspiration, as he was able to benefit from the original symphonies of his "maestro", which he followed faithfully, with a technique excelling Pedrell's.

However, the score of "Fuego Fatuo" was subject to theatrical usage and limitations, and with certain frequency the orchestra doubled the singers'voices, or discovered the way to dispense with them. We must realize that Don Manuel wrote the score first, and the librettist had to mould her poetic and literary talent to the music. Doña María Martínez Sierra was well

Aware of this when she commented "I have never known such an exhausting task as that of inserting or introducing words into previously composed melodies, respecting rhythms, accents and even certain vowels in order to sing them without too much difficulty, while at the same time trying to express the plot clearly and with commonsense. The effort made by the writer can be realized on reading "Fuego Fatuo". As from his very first works, Don Manuel was in favour of the closest possible union between text and music, as in "La vida breve", "El amor brujo", "Canciones" or "El Retablo", perhaps the circumstances surrounding the text for "Fuego" were the reason for his discouragement. This hypothesis is worth bearing in mind.

The revision of such a perfect score appeared to be a highly delicate task. It called for the hand and mind of someone aware of the "metier", who knew the original work, and capable of not misrepresenting Don Manuel's music, even seemingly for the better. The reviser should not leave any personal signs, to the contrary, no-one unaware of his existence should be able to perceive his participation. Antonio Ros Marbá has been 100%

successful in this respect, and his work in setting up Fuego Fatuo, and therefore in memory of Falla, has been outstanding, and indeed exemplary. Anyone who listens to the "Suite sinfónica" can tell me if I am mistaken, and had they not been previously informed, they would not have been able to notice the vocal source of the majority of the pieces.

I must mention a few more things about Falla; it was not his intention to orchestrate a series of pieces. Don Manuel manipulates Chopin's music freely as well as respectfully; he entwines part of one piece with another, returns to the first part, orchestrates it according to the original harmony. or modifies this. The result, however, is one of harmony and perfection. Indeed, it might be said that we are confronted with a present-day concept of orchestration, due to a combination of timbres and a lack of what Don Manuel ironically called "universally accepted" formulas.

Another brief mention: "Fuego Fatuo" is Chopin, but Falla too, an ideal combination. A series of pieces, "Third" from Opus 64, "Second and Fourth Scherzos",

"Mazurkas No. 15 and 25", a Polish song by Chopin-Liszt, "The Berceuse", and "Bolero' or "Tarantela", take on a new lease of life in an artistic act as justified as when the great masters are inspired in the paintings of their predecessors.

The first performance at a public concert of "Fuego Fatuo" was held on 1st July, 1976, at the Granada International Festival, with Antonio Ros Marbá conducting the Nacional Orchestra. The same conductor had previously given a pre-première with the Radio-Television Symphony Orchestra.

VIII. FANTASIA BETICA

Fantasía Bética, intended for Arthur Rubinstein, and the petition received from the Princess of Polignac to write "Retablo de Maese Pedro", quietened the rumours about the Chopin opera, which in view of its purpose, and in spite of its unquestionable artistic quality, was to have no great significance in the aesthetic development of the composer's work, but its contribution was of a marginal nature.

"Fantasía bética" was certainly not Fa-

5

6

lla's finishing work in Andalusian vein. Rubinstein commissioned it, at the same time as another one from Stravinsky, "Piano Rag Music"; this second piece was never performed, and the first one has been played very little. In spite of the Andalusian air inspiring it, the Fantasía was hardly suitable music for the audience of those days. Nevertheless, this is the most important piano music by a Spanish composer since "Iberia" by Albéniz. Falla uses a variety of orchestral resources, incisive and resounding combinations of chords, or a play on diverse planes and melodic sketches of a purely pianistic nature. The composition is far more baroque than in "Piezas españolas", but it is also more interesting, and the value of certain dissonance introduced in a way which is unusual for Falla, is influenced by the timbre of the instruments as well as by the harmony. Falla uses the guitar as a starting point for his work, and this leads him to compose in minor chords in order to suggest the minor tone divisions of the semi-tone so frequently observed in our national instrument. In contrast to the delightful orientation of the piano in "Nights" or the richness of "Piezas", the piano of "Fantasía" depicts the resonant and expressive picture of a serious and deep Andalusia, of a Spain full of violence and contrasts. With time, "Fantasía bética" was fully accepted into his repertoire. However, the very depth of its feelings will be a hindrance to its popularity, as some of his other works.

IX. EL RETABLO DE MAESE PEDRO
(Master Peter's Puppet Show)

The name of Granada summanizes 1920 for Falla. Noew installed in the city of the Alhambra, the composer wrote "Tribute to Debussy", based on "Soirée dans Grenade". Henri Prunière, editor of "Revue Musicale", gave him the idea when he was preparing an issue in honour of Claude of France. Falla wrote a delightful essay for the issue, called "Claude Debussy and Spain", and his guitar "Tribute", with which he also satisfied a long-time petition of a great friend and guitarist, Miguel Llobet. The typical Habana rhythm which Debussy used in his "Soirée" and a change in tune taken from the score, were the allusion to his great friend and master, and leader of the contemporary musical movement in Europe. Don Manuel knew how to compose for that real guitar, representative of the soul and dreams of Spain which Debussy felt, as Falla said, "truly but not genuinely".

Don Manuel was now immersed in the silence of Granada, while at the same time vibrating with the incomparable clarity and light, and alert to the sound of the hidden murmuring water, wandering slowly through the Alhambra woods, and from the top of St. Nicholas contemplating the wonder which appears from among the cypresses, the ancient "red castle". Just as from Paris he dreamt of Andalusia to inspire him with the music of the Generalife or of Cordoba's mountains, in Granada he was attracted by the Castile of Cervantes.

Since his youth, Falla had been attracted by puppet shows. He drew out the parts, made up the puppets and performed the plays to an imaginary audience, as there existed no-one in the corner of his house which the little Manuel called "Eden", except this visionary city, born of his imagination, to which he gave the inspired name of "Colón" (Columbus). Years later, when the young García Lorca wrote his first poems and began to animate the literary atmosphere, Falla rediscovered his interest in puppets. From then onwards Federico took charge of the theatrical side, and Don Manuel the accompaniment. It is quite understandable that when the Princess of Polignac commissioned a play to be performed in her Parisian palace, Falla did not hesitate to adapt an episode from Don Quixote for "Master Peter's puppet show". It was a theatrical form dear to him, and he was challenged by the problem of how to sing adecuately the Castilian Spanish of Cervantes' time.

A considerable number of years previously Falla had attended some lectures in the Ateneo in Madrid, given by the music critic, Don Cecilio de Roda, on the possibility of putting Don Quixote to music. The lectures were published with some musical examples which Falla kept and which he recurred to for some parts of his "Retablo". They were mainly themes by Gaspar Sanz, among them a fanfare which was a starting point for those we can hear in the "Retablo". In other cases the composer has alternated the quixotic atmosphere with that which is represented in the "Retablo", namely the ballad of the Love affair between Don Gayferos and Melisendra. As well as those of Sanz, there are references of Salinas to folk music, such as the "seguidilla" from la Mancha of Master Peter. We can also trace the neo-Scarlattian style in many parts, as the "Sinfonía de Maese Pedro", the central theme of which is from part of the song "De los álamos vengo, madre" (I come from the poplar trees, mother); this was to be further amplified in the first movement of the Concerto. The "Trujuman" (the interpreter with pointer in hand explaining the action of the "Retablo") was particularly difficult. What was most adecuate was a lyrical recital, which would conform with the characteristics of the language and would at the same time appear natural and suitably expressive. Falla made a thorough study of the styles of church music, and its varied repertoire of cadenzas. As well as this he was also interested in a very natural and straightforward form of song, the street proclamations or speeches, which contributed a variety of designs and cadenzas, not to mention the accents and pauses in popular use over the centuries. Nor could he ignore the Spanish ballads, which being essentially narrative, upheld the idea

of clear fluency, and the very intonation and tone of speech that Falla was in search of.

As regards his working method, Falla perfects it in the "Retablo" more than in any of his previous works. A reduced-size orchestra is high-lighted by the introduction of fashionable instruments of the age, the harpsichord and harp-lute, and such is the conciseness of the elements of the orchestra that there is a an exquisite clarity of polyphony, without the necessity for duplication, each instrument or group of instruments playing a dual rôle of sound and harmony. Thanks to this polyphony, even the most apparent dissonance is justified by the play of natural resonance, and those which superficially appear poli-tonal.

The first performance of the "Retablo" was in 1923 in Seville, in concert form, and later as a puppet play in the palace of the Princess of Polignac.

In spite of having renounced his music of Andalusian vein, Manuel de Falla continued his strong defence of the purest form of "cante jondo" (Andalusian folk song). In collaboration with García Lorca, Zuloaga, Andrés Segovia and many other personalities, he organized a competition of "Cante primitivo andaluz" (original Andalusian folk song), which aroused international as well as national interest; the city of the rivers Darro and Genil saw the arrival of critics and musicologists from England, France, Italy, Switzerland and America.

X. CONCERTO PARA CLAVE Y 5 INSTRUMENTOS
(Concerto for Harpsichord and 5 Instruments)

As an outcome of the concerts organized in Seville for the first performance of the "Retablo", Falla founded the Orquesta Bética de Cámara (Andalusian Chamber Orchestra), led by Eduardo Torres and Ernesto Halffter. Don Manuel was equally preoccupied about the development of the orchestra and the musical career of the friend who was later to complete his posthumous work, "Atlántida".

Don Manuel was a firm believer in friendship, and for sentimental reasons gave precedence to everything that was not to the detriment of truth, faith or justice, even though it meant interrupting his musical tasks or his delicate way of life. At the request of one of his great friends, Jean Aubry, between composing "Retablo" and "Concerto", he wrote a small master piece, dedicated to another of his great friendships, Madame Louise Alvar. I am referring to the text of "Psyché" by Jean Aubry, which Falla sets to song accompanied by five instruments, flute, harp, violin, viola and 'cello. The gallantry and XVIIIth century atmosphere suggested in the French verse is evoked by Falla in a very special way: he imagines a court concert held in the "tocador de la Reina" (The Queen's boudoir) in the Alhambra, when in 1730 king Philip V and his wife, Isabel of Farnesio, visited this historical palace in Granada.

Falla wrote to Jean Aubry, author of the text:

Granada, 29th September, 1924

Briefly, my dear Jean, I will recount to you what I am asked about our Psyché:

Philip V and his wife Isabel of Farnesio lived in the Alhambra Palace in 1739.

When I was composing Psyché I imagined a small court concert taking place in the Tocador de la Reina, a high tower overlooking a magnificent panorama, with the interior decorated in contemporary style, as is my music (XVIIIth century Spanish court music), or even better, I have dreamt of this music there.

The Queen's ladies played and sang her a mythological theme, very much in fashion at the time, as we know.

You already know the instruments: flute, harp, violin, viola and 'cello (these last three muted).

The manuscript of the score is 13 pages.

And that is all, for the moment.

In 1923 he began working on the Concerto for harpsichord or piano and five instruments, meant for Wanda Landewska. When it was performed in Paris, Maurice Ravel, on hearing the second movement, exclaimed: "This (page), is the masterpiece of contemporary chamber music". Certainly, we are confronted with another of Falla's compositions which was hardly received with great acclaim to begin with but on account of its intrinsic beauty it will last a long time.

Echoes of Scarlatti are evident in the Concerto from two points of view. One refers to the physiognomy, of which the last movement is an excellent example. Another is the internal texture, in the transformation of small motifs derived from unique bases, and contrary to the dramatic development usual to the Germanic World, Falla has achieved incredible results. Orchestral combination is a risk, particularly if we take into account the fact that the string instruments he uses are not played in an excessive slur form, but by means of sporadic strokes, to achieve harmony or counterpoint.

Like in the central movement, the XVth century Castilian song "I come from the poplars, mother", truly representative of Spanish madrigals of the period, is both the inspiration and the culmination of the first movement. The musical elements previously referred to derive from this same theme, although the composer plays on them from a constructive point of view, as though they were independent themes.

The harpsichord is played with clear arpeggios or long scales, following the style of the vihuela accompaniment to songs in Renaissance times. Pedrell's dreams achieve fulfillment in his disciple's concerto. This abstract music, free of all superfluous description or facile folk references, achieves a fusion of the purist Hispanic values, through which he established not an archaic contribution, but one which is new and exctiting, and which has not suffered devaluation with the passing of time.

In 1926 Wanda Landewska played the harpsichord in the first performance of the concerto in both Barcelona and Switzerland. The following year Falla composed his "sonnet to Córdoba", based on Luis de Góngora's poetry. The most lyrical moments of the "Retablo", or those afterwards brought to us in the "Atlántida", reach a peak in this composition which is grandiose and complete in its melody and in the clarity of the accompanying instrument, in a similar way to the harpsichord in Concerto. 1935 is the date of his "Homenaje a Paul Dukas" (Tribute to Paul Dukas), Falla's maestro in Paris.

XI. AMERICA: HOMENAJES Y ATLANTIDA

In the spring of 1926 Falla travelled to Zurich to take part in the Festival of the Internacional Society of Contemporary Music, and it was then that the creation of "Atlántida" was taking shape in Don Manuel's mind.

The first project consisted of a play about Columbus, taking place in the courtyard of the Alcázar of Seville, for which Paul Claudel wrote the script. The French poet used a dramatic text which was hardly apt for the idea, basically one of mime, conceived by Falla and his artistic designer José María Sert. On the other hand, Don Manuel was considering the idea suggested by Max Reinhardt of setting to music some Spanish eucharistic play. He had chosen "Los encantos de la culpa" (the enchantment of guilt), which attracted Falla for two important reasons: transforming Greek myths into Catholic symbols, and developing the sea theme, together with the presence of Ulysses, "pilgrim of the sea". This "pilgrim" was later to be Falla's title for the last part of "Atlántida".

Granada le 2 9 Septbre
9 2 4

Voici, mon cher Jean, les quelques
lignes que vous me demandez
sur notre Psyché :

Le Philip.. V et sa femme
Isabelle de Parme ont habité
le palais de l'Alhambre en
1 6 3 9 . Or, en composant
Psyché j'ai imaginé un
petit concert de Cour qui au-
rait lieu au Tocador (Boudoir)
de la Reina , qui est une haute
tour (sur un panorama splen-
dide) soit l'intérieur est décoré
dans le style de l'époque, XXXXX
XXXXX qui est aussi celui de ma

musique (musique espagnole
de Cour - XVIIe siècle) ou,
mieux encore : ce que j'ai re-
vé de cette musique là ...

Les Dames de la Reine jouent
et chantent pour elle sur un
sujet mythologique, très à la
mode sous l'époque en ques-
tion comme vous le savez.

Les instruments, vous les
connaissez déjà : Flûte, harpe,
viole-, violes y celles (avec violons,
la partition manuscrite a 13 pages.
Et voilà tout ... pour le moment.

1926, the year in which Falla was 50, also coincided with the 50th year of the great Catalan lyric writer, Jacinto Verdaguer. The composer read parts of his poem, ''Atlántida'', and intermingled with the mythical side, he discovers the epic Spanish achievement of the discovery of America; the sea is the absolute protagonist. He decided to make partial use of Verdaguer's poem, which he would adapt, to give it a more religious emphasis, and at the same time he added other texts, particularly Latin ones, selected from the Holy Bible. In this way he was able to fulfil his fervent ambition to compose church music, a desire which was stimulated by the works of other of our composers of polyphony.

Initially Falla intended to compose a fairly short piece, not longer than half an hour, but his ideas changed and expanded, just as the original idea of scenery became a fusion of music and movement, which Falla and Sert, without any other collaborators, converted into a gigantic historic scene.

Parts of Atlántida were completd by 1928. It is precisely that date which marks the beginning of the most difficult part of the composer's life. His failing health, interruptions on account of other compositions which he was loath to neglect, and the difficult political situation that Spain was undergoing, particularly disturbing to Falla from a religious point of view, and the cruel, drawn-out civil war, made the beginnings of Atlántida slow and costly.

Once the Spanish Civil War had ended, Manuel de Falla accepted the invitation extended by the Spanish Cultural Institute of Buenos Aires to give several recitals of Spanish music, and a first performance of the ''Suite'' and ''Homenajes''; these included one dedicated to Arbós, really a brief fanfare, and those dedicated to Debussy and Dukas, which he adapted for orchestra, and ''Pedrelliana'', based on Pedrell's ''La Celestina'', which he composed in 1938-39, although it had been planned considerably earlier.

In America Falla continued work on Atlántida inso far as his health and other obligations permitted. On several occasions he wrote that if God were to allow him strength to continue for another six months, Atlántida could be finished, and at other times he considered the performance of a partial version, with excepts from Atlántida filling a whole concert programme. The absence of a plastic accompaniment, together with the preoccupation that a concert consisting of excerpts would be unsatisfactory, made him desist from that idea. During this agonizing wait, his spirit immutable, Don Manuel died in Alta Gracia, Córdoba, in the Argentine. His coffin was sent to Spain, and buried in the crypt of Cádiz cathedral, to the murmur of the nearby ''Atlantic''.

After the most meticulous arrangement and revision of the manuscripts left by Falla, Ernest Halffter, his follower, completed the score, which was eagerly awaited by the world. In November of 1961 it was finally performed, as a concert, in Barcelona and Cádiz, and in June of 1962 ''Atlántida'' finally emerged from its long slumber to be staged in the Scala of Milan. In 1976 Halffter arranged a new version, played in the Lucerne Festival, conducted by Jesús López Cóbos.

We can now conclude the chapter on Falla's life and work. As Don Manuel said, ''a musician is yet another worker''; his whole life and profession were dominated by the motto of the Hieronymite monks: ''Honour and Glory are due to God only''.

A great deal has been said and written about ''Atlántida'', and in the future plenty will be said and written about his posthumous works. One important aspect must not be overlooked, namely the extent to which Halffter collaborated with his maestro and exactly what is the significance of Atlántida. Basically, the questions raised by critics stem from a veiled attitude of amazement at that legendary continent presented by Don Manuel in such an introverted and enigmatic way, just as he showed Columbus' imaginary town as a boy.

What makes Atlántida so mysteriously difficult to catalogue, even as a contemporary revised arrangement? Nor must we forget and file it away as a relic of the past. What is the strange power of attraction of this piece of music, which some consider to be a summary of his whole work, and others an insoluble problem? Anyway, Atlántida is an outstanding artistic and human adventure which we can follow through a process which incorporates simplicity and complexity, a combination of expression and of religious introversion, a

PSYCHÉ,

POEME

de Monsieur Jean Aubry, Ecrivain François,

MIS EN MUSIQUE

Par Monsieur DE FALLA, Muficien d'Efpagne,
natif de la Cité de Cadix, en Andaloufie;

De J & W-CHESTER, Editeur pour la Mufique,
à Londres, rue du Grand Marlborough.

M.CM.XXVII.

9

10

great framework formed by microformal elements.

Atlántida is not a theatrical work. Neither its musical development, nor the absence of lyrical participation by the main characters, nor the composer's own wishes point in such a direction. Perhaps it is the conversion of that book of "examples" (which is carried out by means of puppets in the Quixote-like episode), into a great musical book, for solos, choirs and full orchestra, to which is added the fantasy of a great religious altarpiece, as in the impressive cathedral stained-glass windows which Falla admired so much in his journeys through Italy.

Shortly after beginning it, Falla considered Atlántida as his farewell to composing. However, his farewell was to last for twenty years, and the stylistic variations to be found in the music cannot be attributed to the time lapse. This is evident at the very beginning, where there is a variety of styles in, for example, "Atlántida sumergida", "Himno Hispánica" or "Sueño de Isabel". Perhaps it was the composer's intention to cover a whole range, from the purely Iberian impressionism of the Prologue through to the intensely pure and religious finale.

In Atlántida we find a synthesis of all the elements of Falla's musical style from the rest of his work: the primitive type of polyphony of the XIIIth century manuscripts, the characteristics of recitals and ballads, the references to XVIth century composers, the evocation of the sounds of ancient instruments, echoes of military music of times past, the mysticism of certain cadenzas from Lasso to Falla (including Wagner's Parsifal); the good manners of the "gallarda" of the court of Queen Isabel, the descriptive music of the caravels, the distant music of the aparition of the "Angel of Spain", the madrigal-type style reminiscent of Monteverdi, the baroque "hymns" to Spain, to Barcelona, to the Atlántida, or the elegance of the "Pléyades", not forgetting the traditional and popular "sustratum" of Catalonia.

"Atlántida" is a great song in praise of the sea and its mystery, and a deeply religious message of Catholicism. Above all, however, it is the musical work of a free man, of a composer adapted to the times in which he lived, but refusing to submit himself to the prevailing tendencies, and who availed himself of what was convenient, writing freely according to his artistic conscience.

Aesthetic ideology

Manuel de Falla's aesthetic ideas.

INDIVIDUALISM

I am one of those who believe that a true artist should never subscribe to one specific school, however distinguished its qualities. In my modest opinion, individuality is one of the prime virtues that should be demanded of a creative artist.

(1917)

DEBUSSY AND SPAIN

Claude Debussy has written Spanish music without knowing Spain, or rather, without knowing the country, which is quite different. Debussy, who did not really know Spain, quite unconsciously and spontaneously created Spanish music, which was enviable to others who knew Spain only too well. Debussy has executed what

the maestro Felipe Pedrell had already revealed to us about richness of content in our music, and the possibilities deriving from it.

(1920)

FELIPE PEDRELL

Pedrell was a mestro in the strictest sense of the Italian word; he was a constant living example to Spanish musicians of the sure way leading to the creation of a noble and very national art, which at the beginning of the previous century had been believed irreparably lost.

In spite of his constant contacts with the works of our classical composers, and his fervent admiration for them, his own ideas and will-power were strong enough to withstand conventionalities. His aesthetic ideology led him to follow a method, thanks to which the procedures used never exceed in humility the musical essence expressed and enriched. And yet, what richness is concealed behind that apparent modesty, and what an arduous task was entailed discovering the harmony, hidden among popular melodies!

(1923)

USEFULNESS OF ART

I believe in the usefulness as well as the beauty of music from a social point of view. Its composition should not be egoistic, but rather altruistic. To write for an audience without making concessions to them is certainly problematical and is a constant worry to me. We must be worthy of the ideal we conceive, maintain it, and spread it to a maximum; it is an ideal to which we must give expression, and sometimes it takes a great effort, and this effort must be concealed, as though it were an extemporizaction of the greatest ease and simplicity.

(1925)

CENTRES OF ATTRACTION

A purely musical matter; music in which the eternal laws of rhythm and tonality, closely linked, are consciously observed; such a statement does not, however, mean a criticism of those who are honestly working in a different way. To the contrary, I believe that progress in the techniques of a form of art, and the discovery of real possibilities to his expansion, are often due to the use of apparently arbitrary procedures, later subjected to eternal and unchangeable laws.

Everything representing renovation in means of technical expression, although the fulfilment of it is rather more imperfect.

(1925)

AVERSIONS

Fanciful dogmas which become the worst enemies of true and intangible dogmas.

Narrow-minded nationalism.

The use of formulas known as ''of use to the public''.

(1929)

TIME AND SPACE

We must not forget that music develops in a context of time and space, and in order to attract both of them effectively, we must outline them more clearly, establishing clearly the starting point, half-way and terminal points, or the starting point and suspension point, joined by a close internal link, which although sometimes superficially seemingly more distant from the tonal sense accentuated by its limits, is only briefly so, in order to emphasize that same tonal value, which increases in intensity on reappearing, after accidentally becoming eclipsed.

(1933)

RICHARD WAGNER

The co-ordination of his songs and lyrical recitation is true to the expressiveness of the language, apart from some excesses he committed, and this facility he has makes his work supreme, unsurpassed by none.

The influence of Wagner's Germanic characteristics on composers of other nations, including opposing ones, has been discussed at length, which I regret. But to me the case seems clear, treating it justly, far from being detrimental, it has afforded a stimulus whereby composers have made a greater effeort to define and reflect the characteristics of their own nationality in their work.

Nobody previous to Wagner made dramatic action so outstanding in such a favourable musical setting, and in this sense he was an exceptional composer.

(1933)

MAURICE RAVEL

Far from being the "enfant terrible" which many considered him to be in his initial "revealing" stage, I believe Ravel to have been an infant prodigy, whose wonderfully cultured spirit created magical enchantments out of his compositions.

His was a daring art, supremely different, of exquisite perfection, whose procedures of composing, closely linked to the precise selection of sounds, are always true to a creative spirit; his compositions not only reflect his mental activity, born of study as well as experience, but also an inspiration which is beyond that attainable by purely human means.

Ravel's genius, far from being simply lively and ingenious, as Gracian tells us, and others also corroborate, reveals the hidden strength impelling it. His choice of latent harmonic resonance, as indeed of his orquestra, of such nebulous elasticity and such vibrations, is sufficient to refute that impassivity which can superficially be attributed to this musician, and which I think should be attributed to an unconscious reticence on his part. I feel it is unnecessary to insist on my theories of the

deep sensitivity of this infant prodigy, which is apparent throughout his music; the same sensitivity is also revealed in the accentuation and unmistakable inflexion of his lyrical recitation.

(1939)

CANTE "JONDO" (Andalusian gipsy singing)

This name is given to a group of Andalusian songs, the most genuien of which seems to be the gipsy "siguiriya", which has been the source for many others, still conserved; which, together with "polos", "martinetes" and "soleares", have highly distinctive qualities which differentiate them from other types of singing within that all-embracing popular name of "flamenco".

Stricly speaking, this latter name should really only be applied to the more modern group of songs which includes "malagueñas", "granadinas", "rondeñas" (origin of the first two types), "sevillanas", "peteneras", etc., which can only be considered as derivations of the previous group.

The gipsy "siguiriya" is recognized as a class of song within the "cante jondo" group, but before underlining its value from a purely musical point of view, we should indicate that this Andalusian singing is the only European one which maintains both structurally and stylistically the highest qualities inherent in primitive singing of oriental civilizations.

(1922)

THE GUITAR

Popular guitar-playing represents two definite musical values, obvious and immediate rhythm, and purely tonal-harmonic value.

The former, together with some easilyassimilated cadenzas, has been the only aspect for a long time used in artistic playing, whereas the second aspect, that of its purely tonal harmonic value, has sacarcely been recognized by composers, with the exception of Scarlatti, until a relatively short time ago.

"Jondo" playing is unrivalled in Europe. The harmonic effects unconsciously achieved by our guitarists are one of trewonders of natural art. What is more, it is believed that our XVth century musicians were probably the first harmonic accompanists (with chords) of vocal or instrumental melody.

(1922)

INDEX OF WORKS

Pages from Youth (1889-1904)

Quartet with piano (Andante and Scherzo).
Fantasy for quintet, on "Mireya", by Mistral.
Melody for 'cello and piano.
Andalusian serenade for piano.
Cappricho Walts, for piano.
Nocturne, for piano.
"Tus ojillos negros" (Your little black eyes), song, words by Cristóbal de Castro.
"Limosna de amor", (Alms of love), light opera, book by Jackson Veyan.
"El Cornetín de órdenes" (the Bugler), light opera, with A. Vives.
"La Cruz de Malta", (The Cross of Malta), light opera, with A. Vives.
"La Casa de Tócame Roque", light opera on the book by Ramón de la Cruz.
"Los amores de la Inés", light opera, book by Emilio Duggi.

Adult compositions:

La vida breve (The Brief Life), book by Carlos Fernández-Shaw. (1904-1905).
Cuatro Piezas Españolas (Four Spanish Pieces), for piano, (1908).
Tres melodías (Three melodies), text by Théophile Gautier (1909) Noches en los jardines de España (Nights in the Gardens of Spain), for piano and orchestra, (1911-1915).
Siete canciones populares españolas (Seven popular Spanish songs), for voices and piano (1914).
Oración de las madres que tienen a sus hijos en brazos (Prayer for mothers with babes in arms), text by Martínez Sierra, for voices and piano (1914).
El amor brujo (Bewitched Love), ballet, plot by Martínez Sierra, (1914-1915).
El Sombrero de tres picos, (The three-cornered hat), ballet, plot by Alarcón-Martínez Sierra, 1918-1919.
Fuego Fatuo, (Will-o-The-wisp), comic opera based on Chopin, unpublished, (1919).
Fantasía Bética (Iberian Fantasy), for piano, (1919).
Homenaje a Debussy (Tribute to Debussy), for guitar, (1920). El retablo de Maese Pe-

dro (Master Peter's Puppet Show), musical adaptation and setting of an episode from Don Quixote, (1919-1922).

Psyché, for voices and four instruments, text by J. Aubry, 1929.

Concerto para clave (o piano) y cinco instrumentos, (Harpsichord and five-instrument concert), (1923-26).

Soneto a Córdoba, (Sonnet to Córdoba) for voices and harp, poems by Luís de Góngora, (1927).

Fanfare to the name of Arbós, (1934).

Homenaje a Paul Dukas, (Tribute to Paul Dukas) for piano, (1935).

Homenajes, (Tributes), suite for orchestra, (1939).

Atlántida, for solos, choirs, orchestra, based on Verdaguer, completed by Ernesto Halffter (1927-1960).

New versión, (1976).

FOOTNOTES

1. See ''Larga historia de 'La vida breve''' (Long History of 'The Brief Life''' by Guillermo Fernández-Shaw (Madrid).

2. Manuel García Matos: ''Folklore in Falla'', (Magazine: ''Música'', Madrid.)

3. See E. Franco: ''Atlántida, long adventure'', Ricordi, Milan, 1961.

MUSICAL CHRONICLES

MANUEL DE FALLA, IN GRANADA.

fter wandering up thourgh the wonderful gardens and the impressive Gate of Justice, the finely balanced proportions of the Gate of Wine evoke the emotional memory of the ''prelude'', in which the French genius sang about it, visualizing it in his imagination. A little further up, and at the end of a row of houses gathered on the top of the Alhambra hill, we find Manuel de Falla's rustic retreat, the brilliance of white-washed walls broken by the blue door and windows. The interior is of the utmost simplicity, and quiet, good taste, with a hint of influence of Zuloaga, for instance in the rush half-panelling on the walls, held in place with huge old nails, against which the blue of the furniture stood out remarkably.

The room was tinged with an orange light filtering through the striped, Alpujarra curtains, and a big porcelain jug gleamed in one corner. Ripe quinces and pomegranates blocked out the distant dihouette of the Sierra Nevada, and the cypresses of the Generalife could barely be discerned through the intertwined jazmin. The heavy heat of October seems bearable under the dense roof of creeping vines, with the accompaniment of a nearby, murmuring fountain. This seems almost poetic, maestro, doesn't it? Falla smiles and half closes his eyes. Throughout those long years in Paris, Falla's illusion was to live in Granada; now he seemed to be living in a dream world. There are a thousand different images of the Sierra Nevada, the fertile valley which seems to disappear into the horizon, like an imaginary sea at dusk, reflecting a myriad of stars in its shining surface, and they create a sense of peace and calm, engulfing his mind and spirit.

''Each night when I go to bed'', he says, ''I am struck by new ideas and projects, and in each of them I would like to renew my techniques, my procedures, every facet, to reflect a new tone; changes which confirm my personality, new approaches and new points of view.''

Repetition, old age and conformity are a danger! The secret is renewal, in such a way that this should define in every different position the total volume that a statue draws in space: basic unity and physical plurality. Until now, few artists have been able to accomplish this magnificent aim.

Adolfo Salazar
Sol, 25th October, 1921.

Para mis hijos.

Salida de D. Manuel de Falla de su casa de Granada,
Antequeruela Alta nº. 11.

En la casa de D. Manuel de Falla el día 28 de Septiembre
de 1939 nos reunimos, a las 3 de la tarde, varios amigos de Don
Manuel para despedirlo con motivo de su viaje a Buenos Aires.
Estuvimos D. Ramón Pérez de Roda y su esposa Dña. Eugenia,
Dña. María Prieto de Olóriz y una Srta. prima suya, Dña. Eloísa Morell de
Gallego Burín, alcalde de Granada; la Srta. Emilia Llanos, una Srta. que des-
conozco, D. Pedro Borrajo y su hija, D. Luis Jiménez y el que esto escri-
be Hermenegildo Lanz y su esposa Dña. Sofía Durán de Lanz.
También estaban D. Germán Falla, su esposa y su hija Mari-bel. En
el patio una ancianita a la que atiende en su sustento María del Carmen Falla, una servidora y otra mujer de la vecindad.
En el reducido comedor de la casa, entre maletas y baúles, hacíamos
tertulia en torno a María del Carmen que no creía en el viaje y pen-
saba que no lo haría. La conversación general carecía de inte-
rés, el ingenio se debatía entre vulgaridades impropias de la inte-
ligencia de la mayoría de los asistentes. Hay momentos en que los
cerebros se acorchan y las palabras no expresan más que tonterías
inexplicables.
Sobre las tres y media baja de las habitaciones D. Manuel, seguido
de su hermano Germán y de su cuñada. María del Carmen se des-
pide de sus amigas besándolas y de los amigos estrechando sus ma-
nos, a mí me concede el honor de un abrazo...¡Dios se lo pague!
La emoción contenida a duras penas tiene un momento de expan-
sión en ambos pero se reprime al instante. Es una santa María
del Carmen, para ella soy un hermano más, para mí es casi
una madre. No cambiamos ni una palabra, ni adiós siquiera.
Sigue despidiéndose y entra con los ojos ligeramente húmedos, en
el auto, pero con expresión sonriente, como de quien no va le-
jos y piensa regresar pronto.
Don Manuel sigue a su hermana, a todos va dando la mano, a
todos les dice adiós...—¡Adiós, hasta pronto! va diciendo, con su cara de
santo anacoreta y su expresión bondadosa, sonriente pero pálido,
muy pálido, animado sin embargo y queriendo animar a los de-
más. No tardó mucho tiempo en despedirse de cuantos está-

Document from Hermenegildo Lanz, describing
Manuel de Falla's departure from Granada.

ban en el comedor. En el patio aguardábamos varias personas después del breve instante de la despedida de Maria del Carmen. Don Manuel se acercó a mí, le abracé con la mayor ternura y le dije al oído debilmente...¡gracias...muchas gracias!. No me abrazó, y me lo dijo, porque no puede mover los brazos con soltura, por la operación quirúrgica sufrida pero inclinó su cara sobre mi cara y sentí su emoción, no reprimida como la de su hermana sino expresada con palabras tan terribles, profundas y distintas a las anteriores que las recojo porque me hirieron en lo más hondo de mi alma. — ¡Adios, hasta la Eternidad, en el fondo del mar, tal vez. Lo que sea voluntad de la Providencia!.........................

Adios... (se despedía, dándoles la mano, de la ancianita, la servidora y la vecina) hasta la Eternidad, allí nos volveremos a encontrar todos; en el fondo del mar estaré solo, es lo mismo, no importa lo que sea voluntad de la Providencia!... Estas tres mujeres lloraban... ¡No, Señorito!— decían y D. Manuel, andando con más ligereza que la habitual y con la cara encendida de color, con los ojos brillantes y la sonrisa expresiva, ¡nerviosamente expresiva! tomó asiento en el coche, al lado derecho de su hermana, recibiendo allí el beso más puro de su sobrinita Mari-bel.

Todos los amigos de D. Manuel en otros tiempos mutuamente buenos amigos, nos despedimos al instante unos de otros, seguramente, para no reunirnos más....

¡Que le vamos a hacer, nos reuniremos en la Eternidad!......

H. Jauri

A las 7 de la tarde del mismo día de la partida. En mi estudio.

— Después de escrita esta impresión me acosté porque sentía frío, de toda la tarde, bastante malestar y disgusto y hoy, día siguiente, después de dormir muy mal, de apenas dormir, cuento las horas desde que se marchó mi segundo padre D. Manuel de Falla, el hombre que modeló mi espíritu, quizá para no volverlo a ver jamás.

Cúmplase la voluntad de Dios!.

29-IX-1.939

Index of Illustrations

1. *Title page of the first edition of "Vida Breve", Paris, 1913. Drawn by his brother Germán.*

2. *In the Patio de los Leones with Massine in 1916.*

3. *Portrait of Falla by Picasso, Paris, 9th June, 1920.*

4. *Russian Ballet, Madrid 1921. With Falla are Robert Delaunay, Boris Kochno, Igor Stravinski, Sonia Delaunay, Sergei Diaghilew and Randolfo Barochi.*

5. *Landowska and Falla in Granada, November 1922. With them are Francisco García Lorca, Antonio Luna, Mª del Carmen de Falla, Federico García Lorca, Wanda Landowska and José Segura.*

6. *Photographed with Andrés Segovia in the Carmen de la Antequerela. About 1924.*

7. *Manuel de Falla, aged 50. (1926)*

8. *Parchment drawn by Hermenegildo Lanz, with the city nomination of Falla as Honorary Citizen of Granada.*

9. *Title page of Psyche. Text by G.J. Awbry. Music by Manuel de Falla, composed in Granada in 1924. Commentary by Manuel de Falla on the subject on a separate page.*

10. *Visit to Granada by Alfredo Casella and the "Trio Casella" in 1924. In front of the lion of the Partal: Arturo Bonucci (Cello), Leopoldo Torres Balbás (Architect), Manuel de Falla, Arrigo Serato (Violinist) and Alfredo Casella (Composer and pianist).*

11. *Manuel de Falla shakes hands with "Don Quixote", S.I.M.C. Festival. Venice 1932.*

12. *Manuel de Falla with Vicente Escudero on the balcony of his Granada studio, summer 1933.*

Index

*The
third edi-
tion was prin-
ted on 31sr july,
1988, being the day
of Saint Ignacio Loyola,
by "Meridional Impresores,
S. C. And." the text has been
printed with "Garamond 10" letters.
Using "138 gr./m2" paper. The design
and supervision of the edition
has been carried out by
Julio Juste.*

Translation by
D.L. Kelham

Photographs in colour
J. Garrido y J. Algarra

Black and white photographs
Manuel de Falla ARCHIVES

Official registry nº:
GR. 877/1988

*Manuel de Falla's
House and
Museum*